MOTORCYCLES

Design   Cooper – West
Editor   Denny Robson
Researcher Cecilia Weston-Baker
Illustrator   Rob Shone

Consultant   Howard Lees, BSc,
Member Institute Mechanical
Engineering, UK

Designed and produced by
Aladdin Books Ltd
70 Old Compton Street
London W1

*First Published in the
United States in 1986 by*
Franklin Watts
387 Park Avenue South
New York NY 10016

ISBN 0 531 10200 9

Library of Congress Catalog
Card Number: 86 50033

Printed in Belgium

MODERN
TECHNOLOGY

MOTORCYCLES

JULIAN RYDER

FRANKLIN WATTS
NEW YORK · LONDON · TORONTO · SYDNEY

The Elf Endurance racer, stripped of its bodywork

Foreword

A hundred years ago, motorcycles were simply ordinary pedal bikes fitted with small, crude engines. However, over the years, steady technical development has changed these early unreliable boneshakers into sophisticated and powerful modern machines, of an immense variety. There are now motorcycles catering to every taste, in all shapes and sizes, powered by engines from under 50cc to nearly 1500cc.

Today, motorcycle engineers and designers are making dramatic technological advances, producing machines whose performance, handling and pollution records, comparable with the most expensive sports car, make them some of the most exciting vehicles you can see.

Contents

Today's motorcycle

While the car has undergone vast changes over the last century, the basic concept of the motorcycle has not changed very much. It has been traditionally considered a more functional machine. But with the rapid advancement in motorcycle design over the last ten years, we are now seeing motorcycles that are extremely sophisticated, powerful and comfortable, with features that take advantage of modern technology from many areas.

Today's motorcycles can be turbocharged, have electronic ignition and fuel injection, water-cooled engines and adjustable air suspension. Also, quiet machines that produce little pollution have given motorcycles a less antisocial image.

2 Suspension and brakes

Some of today's motorcycles use a computer to control air suspension. Both front forks and rear suspension are adjustable for a wide range of riding conditions and loads. Modern motorcycles also use disk brakes, which are more efficient and lighter than ever before.

3 Tires and wheels

Modern wheels are lightweight castings of aluminum or magnesium alloy. They are much stronger than the earlier spoked design and they carry wide, low-profile tires. Wheels are now as small as 40cm (16in) in diameter, which means they create less air resistance and they corner better.

1 Electronics

Small microcomputers are used to control and monitor engines that use fuel injection and turbochargers. The amount of fuel used and the timing of the ignition spark are varied according to information from sensors in the engine.

Kawasaki GPZ1000RX

Performance

Bikes are smaller and lighter than ever before. And yet the latest generation of sporting 250cc engines can reach speeds in excess of 190 km/h (120 mph). They are easy to ride on the road, yet capable of winning on the race track.

The Kawasaki GPZ1000RX is a good example of the type of motorcycle mass-manufacturers are producing today, and uses technology that was previously found only in very expensive hand-built motorcycles or racing bikes.

4 The engine
Modern multi-cylinder engines produce a lot of power. Engines as small as 750cc can spin at more than 11,000 revolutions per minute and produce over 100 brake horsepower. More power means more heat and water-cooling is now standard to get rid of this heat. The engine can therefore run more efficiently, giving more power over a greater spread of engine speeds.

5 Frame
The old bicycle steel loop frame has been replaced by a variety of designs often made from aluminum tubing. The very strong main engine casings can be used as a part of the frame to take some of the load. This saves a lot of weight and space.

6 Aerodynamics and materials
Fairings not only protect the rider, they help to streamline the motorcycle. This assists both speed and fuel economy. Materials such as carbon fiber and aluminum are being used to save weight.

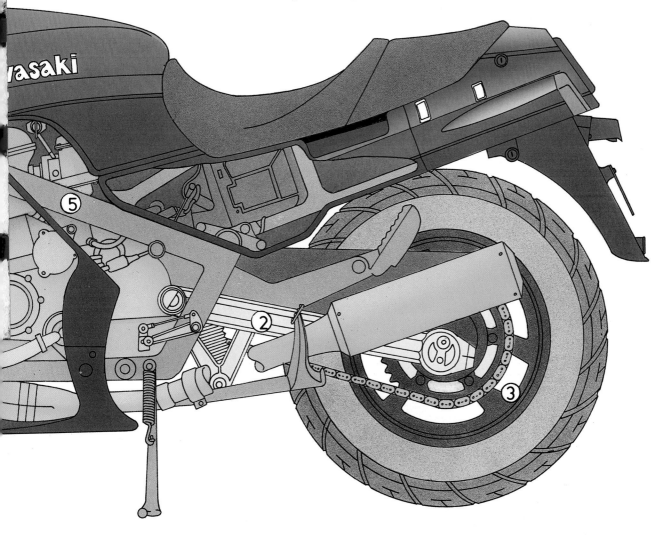

Speed, comfort or economy?

Motorcycles come in a great variety of shapes and types. If you want speed, there are motorcycles like the GSX-R Suzukis, which are racers with lights and silencers. If you need to cover long distances comfortably with a passenger and luggage, a cruiser like the enormous Honda Gold Wing or Yamaha Venture would be appropriate. For short distances, there is the town bike, like the Honda 50 Cub, the world's top selling motorcycle, or the more complex Honda Vision. These motorcycles have automatic gearboxes, electric starters, good weather protection and low running costs. They are designed for people who need inexpensive transportation, as opposed to the enthusiast who buys bigger and more powerful motorcycles.

▽ The Yamaha FZ750 is a typical superbike. It wins races on the tracks but is also at home touring on the roads.

▷ The 50cc Honda Vision is a complex bike, designed to be easy to ride for the commuter or shopper.

Cruisers

The biggest motorcycles available are the cruisers. They have big engines to carry vast amounts of luggage, enormous fairings and many gimmicks. No cruiser is complete without stereo, CB radio, on-board computer and lots of chrome and extra instruments. This fashion originated in the USA, as did the custom bike. Originally owners chopped all the surplus weight off their motorcycles to give a stripped down appearance – hence the word "chopper." Today, factories reproduce this look on the production line with motorcycles that have high handlebars, a small tank, a stepped seat and a small, fat back wheel.

▽ In the photographs below are two types of cruiser. On the left is a Honda Gold Wing, fully loaded with accessories. On the right is a Harley-Davidson factory-produced "chopper."

▷ One of the most popular accessories fitted to cruisers is the cruise control. This device holds the bike at a constant cruising speed, so that the rider can enjoy more comfortable long-distance journeys. As illustrated in the diagram, sensors are linked to a control unit – a micro-computer. Once the control is set, the bike will automatically maintain that speed, even up or down hill. If the rider has to brake or accelerate, the cruise control cuts out until the maneuver is over.

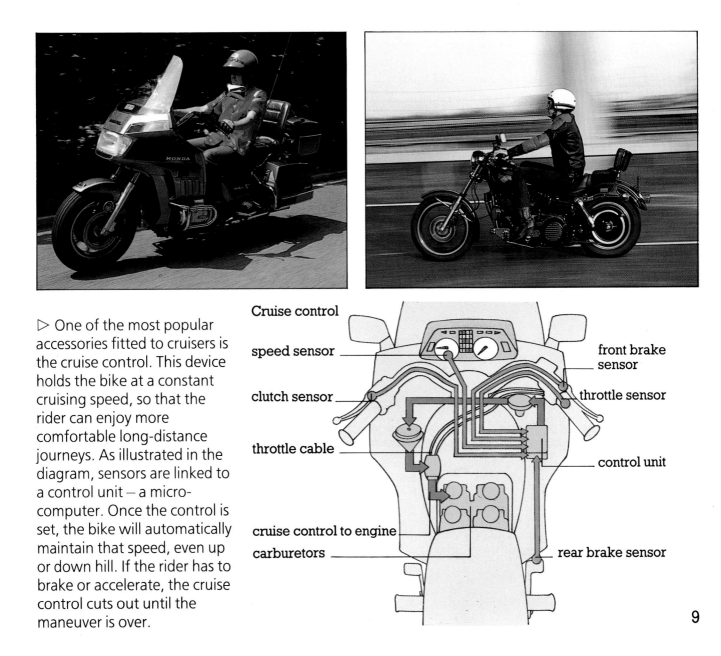

Cruise control

speed sensor

clutch sensor

throttle cable

cruise control to engine

carburetors

front brake sensor

throttle sensor

control unit

rear brake sensor

Inside the engine

Modern engines can be two-stroke or four-stroke. Each cylinder sucks in a mixture of air and fuel and uses the spark plug to ignite it. The burning gas expands and pushes the piston down, turning the crankshaft and eventually driving the rear wheel. Today, engines use two, three, four or six cylinders, because the moving parts, pistons, valves and con rods, are smaller. The parts can be made of aluminum and titanium alloys, which are light and let the engine spin faster.

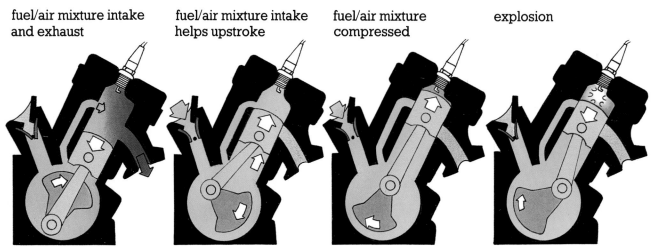

fuel/air mixture intake and exhaust

fuel/air mixture intake helps upstroke

fuel/air mixture compressed

explosion

downstroke

upstroke

△ In a two-stroke engine, there are two strokes of the piston for every explosion. The fuel/air mixture is ignited, pushing the piston down the barrel. The expanding gas escapes out of the exhaust port as it is uncovered. Meanwhile, the mixture in the crankcase is compressed until the transfer port is uncovered. Then the compressed mixture in the crankcase is squirted into the cylinder, pushing exhaust gases out. The piston goes back up. The vacuum caused below the piston sucks in fresh mixture.

Two-stroke engines

Two-stroke engines have fewer moving parts than four-stroke engines, as they do not need valves and camshafts. This means that they are easier to produce and maintain and that they are smaller than four-stroke engines. The fuel used is a mixture of oil and gasoline and is burned after it has done its job. They are more powerful than a four-stroke engine of the same size, but use more fuel and make more smoke.

▷ Like cars, the latest four-stroke engines have multi-valve cylinders. This is a Yamaha FZ750 engine with the cylinder head detached, showing the three inlet and two exhaust valves. The valves let the engine pack the maximum amount of fuel/air mixture into the cylinder in the shortest time.

fuel/air intake   fuel/air mixture compression   explosion   exhaust

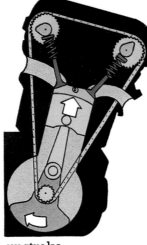

downstroke   upstroke   downstroke   upstroke

△ In a four-stroke engine there are four strokes of the piston for every explosion. On the intake stroke, fuel/air mixture is sucked in through the inlet valve by the piston going down. On the compression stroke, the piston returns and compresses the mixture as both valves are closed.
The spark plug ignites the mixture which explodes and pushes the piston back down the cylinder. The piston travels back up the cylinder pushing burned gases out through the open exhaust valve.

Four-stroke engines

Most multi-cylinder engines are four-strokes. The four-stroke is a more complex piece of machinery than the two-stroke, because there are more moving parts, with arrangements of three, four and even five valves per cylinder! And the valves and their camshafts on top of the cylinder make four-strokes much taller. Unlike two-strokes, the four-stroke engine has its own lubricating oil, which is changed regularly.

Engine layouts

Manufacturers have used every imaginable type
of cylinder layout since the first single-cylinder
motorcycle. Some arrangments are an attempt to
get weight low down in the frame for better
handling. But others are just for variety.

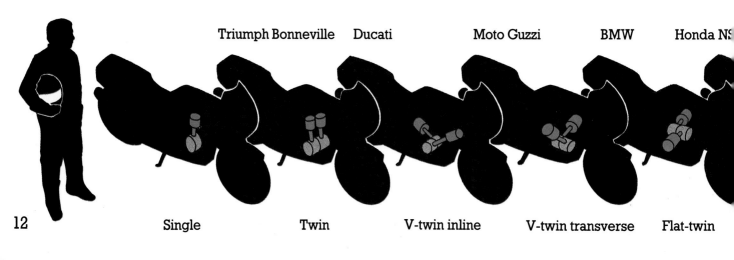

Triumph Bonneville   Ducati   Moto Guzzi   BMW   Honda NS

Single   Twin   V-twin inline   V-twin transverse   Flat-twin

Complexity equals expense

Arrangements like Honda's V-four engines manage to pack a lot of engine into a small space. But because there are two banks of cylinders, there must be two camchains, two sets of camshafts and of course two sets of barrels and cylinder heads. The higher and wider straight-four needs only one set of these parts and is therefore cheaper to manufacture. Suzuki's square-four RG500 racer and Gamma streetbike have two crankshafts. The engine is effectively two parallel twins geared together. Modern, complicated designs tend to cost more money than the old types.

National characteristics

Certain arrangements are associated with certain companies or countries. The British industry dominated motorcycling with the parallel twin engine for almost 25 years. Japan has done the same with the straight four, while the Italian industry has made the V-twin its trademark.

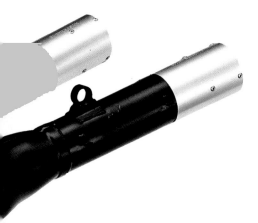

◁ Shown here is a Suzuki RG500 engine. It is a water-cooled, square-four, two-stroke engine. Such a compact design is essential to modern motorcycles.

▽ An engine can give a bike distinction in the same way that styling can. The engine arrangements below suggest certain models or makes.

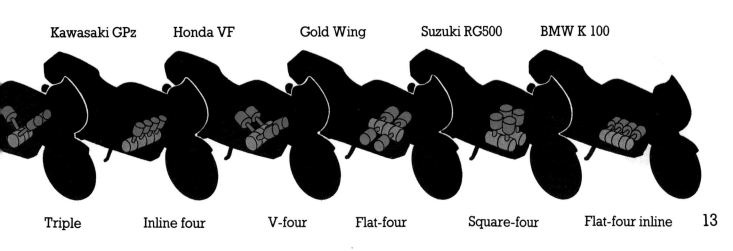

| Kawasaki GPz | Honda VF | Gold Wing | Suzuki RG500 | BMW K 100 |

| Triple | Inline four | V-four | Flat-four | Square-four | Flat-four inline |

The engine at work

Today, motorcycles have the highest power output for their size of any vehicle. Road engines are now more powerful than racing engines were a few years ago. And new techniques have been used to produce plenty of power at any engine speed, while still meeting strict noise and pollution limits.

Variable valve gear

Two-stroke engines now have special power valves that adjust the opening and closing of the exhaust port to suit the engine speed. This lets the engine work properly at low as well as at high revs. Honda's "REVS" system opens both inlet valves in each cylinder at high speed, but only one valve when the engine is spinning slower, to save fuel and make it more efficient.

▷ This is a simplified diagram of what happens inside a water-cooled, four-stroke engine. The fuel/air mixture is green and the exhaust gas is red. The carburetor mixes gasoline and air, which is sucked into the combustion chamber. When this mixture burns, a lot of heat is created. Oil is used to carry heat away from the hot engine, as well as to lubricate moving parts. It is pumped up to the valves and the crankshaft bearings, and then flows back down to the sump. Water is used to do the rest of the cooling. It too is pumped to the hot parts of the engine and then through a radiator.

water   oil   gasoline   air   exhaust

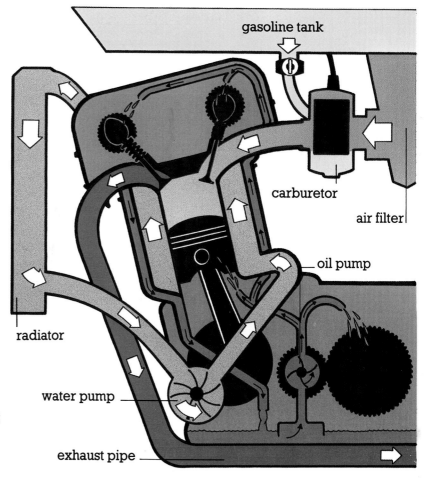

gasoline tank

carburetor

air filter

oil pump

radiator

water pump

exhaust pipe

New technology

Microcomputers are used in most bikes now to control ignition timing, fuel injection systems or power valves. Sensors monitor air flow, engine speed, throttle opening, load and temperature and adjust all the systems for the best results. To keep noise down, engines can have covers lined with noise insulation material. Special filters, "catalytic converters," in the exhaust pipes of two-stroke engines remove harmful pollutants. And balance weights cancel out vibration and make the latest engines very smooth and quiet.

△ This is a Yamaha turbo bike. Turbochargers use the exhaust gas to spin a pump that pushes extra fuel/air mixture into the cylinder under pressure. This gives a lot of extra power. At the moment they are only being used with limited success. However they may yet become as popular on bikes as they are on trucks and cars.

Fuel injection

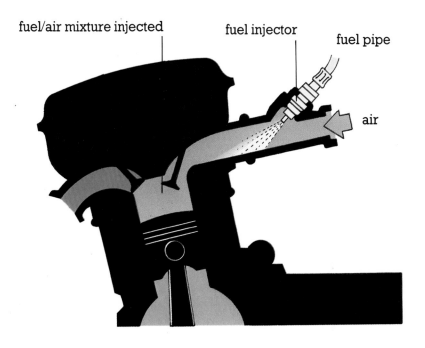

fuel/air mixture injected

fuel injector

fuel pipe

air

◁ Fuel injectors are an alternative to carburetors, and are used on BMW's K-series machines and Honda's, Suzuki's and Kawasaki's turbo bikes. The injector is simply a nozzle that can squirt a variable amount of gasoline into the inlet, where it mixes with air before going into the cylinder head. The injectors are electronically controlled by a small computer that will decide how much gasoline to use, depending on information from sensors.

The drive train

Power from the engine finds its way to the rear wheel through a clutch, gearbox and final drive. Today's clutches need to cope with high engine power and are hydraulically operated. Some small motorcycles have automatic clutches that engage as the throttle is opened.

The gearbox lets the engine turn at the right speed for all conditions, and motorcycles have up to six gears. Usually a foot lever is used to change gear, but some motorcycles have automatic gearboxes.

Shaft, chain or belt drive

From the gearbox, drive goes to the rear wheel through a shaft, chain or belt. Shaft drive is expensive, but unlike chain drive, it never needs adjusting. However, chain is still the most popular method. Small motorcycles have used belt drive for years, but some now have special pulleys that change size, altering the gearing to suit the speed of the bike and so eliminating the need for a gearbox. Some larger motorcycles now have toothed rubber belts instead of chains. These last much longer, do not need any lubrication and are very quiet.

▽ The photograph of this Maico GM500 motocross bike clearly shows the chain running from the gearbox to the rear wheel. The latest chains last a long time, because grease is kept inside the chain by little rubber seals.

▽ The diagram below illustrates how the drive train works on a Yamaha XJ900. A gear on the right-hand end of the crankshaft drives another gear on the back of the clutch drum. These are called the primary gears. The clutch can then pass drive to the gearbox or disconnect it from the back wheel. The shaft that carries the clutch is the mainshaft; the other is the layshaft. Each shaft carries five gears. The gear lever selects which of these pairs transmits drive to the shaft. The gear on the end of the drive shaft then turns the gear in the wheel.

△ The photograph shows a Kawasaki GPZ305 which uses belt drive. The use of reinforced rubber belts is the latest development in final drive. However, their pulleys have to be very wide and so take up a lot of space.

pistons

primary drive

clutch

gearbox

clutch lever

crankshaft

gear lever

universal joint

shaft

cogged wheel

17

Wheels, tires and brakes

Today's superbikes use cast aluminum or magnesium alloy wheels. These are very strong and light, and because there are no holes for spokes, tubeless tires can be used. Honda uses wheels built up from aluminum alloy sections, and uses the same type of wheel made from carbon fiber on its racing bikes. Spoked wheels are still used on motocross bikes because they are more flexible and absorb heavy shocks.

Smaller wheels give better streamlining and quicker steering, and wide, low-profile tires are used to give better grip. Radial tires run cooler and give better roadholding as well as longer life on big motorcycles. Racing bikes use "slick" tires for even better grip in dry conditions.

▽ The photograph shows a racing bike with low-profile "slicks." These are bald treadless tires. They give maximum grip, but only in dry conditions, by putting a wide contact patch of rubber on the road. The inset clearly shows the slick front tire, with twin disks, drilled for lightness.

△ This strange-looking tire is used on an ice-racing bike and the spikes are the only way the wheel can find grip. They look very dangerous, but they let the bike lean over so far that the rider's elbow scrapes the track. Motocross and other off-road machines use tires with pronounced lumps. They come in a variety of shapes for different types of ground.

Disk brakes

Today, most bikes over 400cc use two front and one rear disk brakes. Disks can be ventilated and in the case of racing bikes, be made of aluminum or carbon fiber.

Brake calipers can have four pistons to put more pressure on the brake pad, and magnesium and titanium are used on some calipers to save weight. Motorcycles will soon have anti-lock brakes as a standard feature, allowing riders to stop quickly on wet or icy roads without skidding.

▷ The hydraulic disk brake is really a very simple device. When the brake lever is squeezed, hydraulic fluid moves the pistons in the caliper inward. The pistons push the friction pads against the disk. As the disk is attached to the wheel, this slows the motorcycle down. Disks can be drilled for lightness and to help in clearing water off the brake.

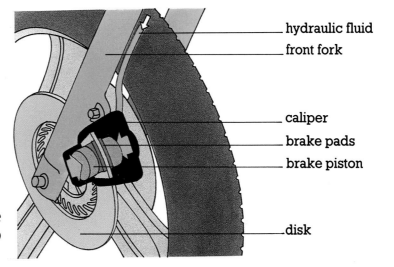

hydraulic fluid
front fork
caliper
brake pads
brake piston
disk

Suspension

For a motorcycle to handle properly when braking, accelerating or cornering, good suspension is vital. It is also very important for the rider's comfort. Modern motorcycles have even more sophisticated suspension than expensive sports cars.

Adjustable springing

Today, air and springs are adjustable for load and firmness of spring rate. Damping can be adjusted separately in each direction, and large remote reservoirs keep the damping oil cool. A "damper" is something used to stop the wheels going up and down like a yo-yo. Nitrogen gas is used to pressurize the damper units to keep them working smoothly under all conditions. Many motorcycles now have the front suspension linked to the braking system, to compensate automatically for forward weight transfer when the brakes are used hard.

▽ The photograph below shows the front forks compressed as the rider negotiates the rough terrain. The diagram shows a telescopic fork leg, which contains the fork spring, damper, damping oil and an air gap at the top. When the leg is compressed, the spring is compressed and oil is forced through the damper to slow movement down. The air is also compressed and acts like an extra spring.

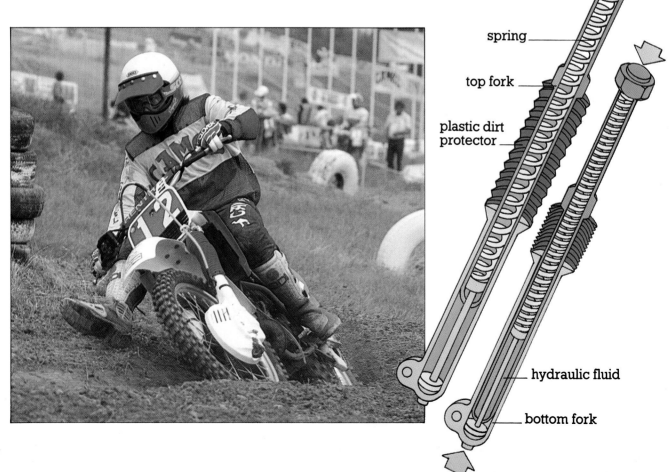

air

spring

top fork

plastic dirt protector

hydraulic fluid

bottom fork

suspension

frame

swingarm

linkages

swingarm moves up

suspension compressed

△ Motocross and road bikes now use a single rear suspension unit linked to the swingarm via a series of levers. This is arranged to give what is called "rising rate" suspension, illustrated above. The swingarm can move easily at the start of its travel, but the further it rises, the harder is the resistance from the suspension unit. In practice, this means that small ripples can be soaked up easily and big bumps can also be absorbed. The photograph of the motocross bike in mid-air (left) clearly shows the single rear suspension unit at its full extension, which will be needed when the bike lands!

▷ Cruisers take the idea of air suspension to the limit. Rear suspension relies totally on air to act as the spring. The Honda Aspencade and Yamaha Venture (illustrated) even have an on-board pump that can raise or lower the air pressure inside the front forks and rear suspension unit automatically. A push-button panel inside the fairing operates the pump and an electronic display tells the rider what pressures he is using.

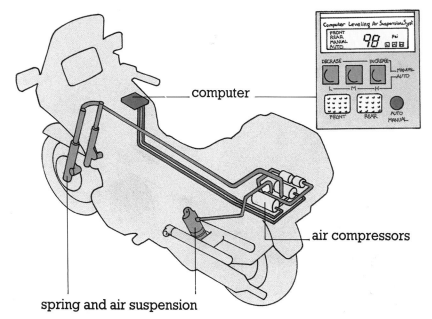

computer

air compressors

spring and air suspension

Frames and new materials

The frame has to form a rigid link between the working parts of a motorcycle. The steering head, swingarm pivot and the engine must be kept in the same position relative to each other, or the handling will suffer.

A triangle is the stiffest shape known to man, and the best frames are built up from a series of triangles joined together. Sometimes the engine is used to form one or two sides of the triangle. The Elf experimental racing bike actually uses the engine as the complete frame, bolting the steering head and swingarm to each end.

▽ Yamaha's "Lateral Frame Concept" is an advanced loop type frame, of rectangular section and round tubing. It supports the steering head by wrapping around in front of it.

▽ Honda's "beam" frame for the new VFR750 uses a single box section beam running each side of the narrow V-four engine from steering head to swingarm pivot. The engine forms one side of a triangle.

▽ Bimota's DB1 frame uses a "backbone" made from straight lengths of round tubing forming a stiff, triangulated structure. The engine is suspended under the frame.

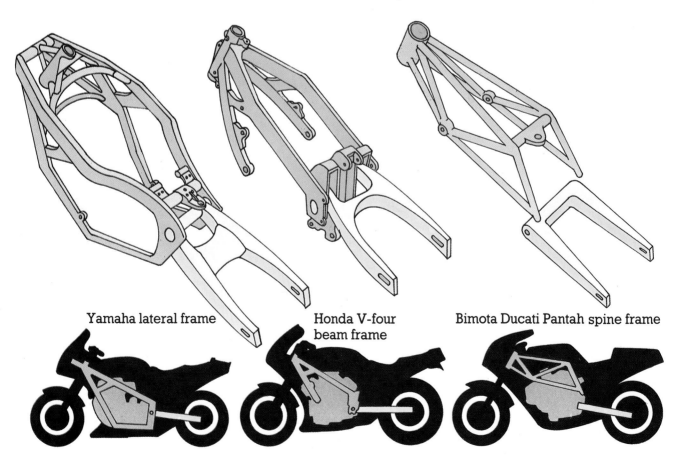

Yamaha lateral frame

Honda V-four beam frame

Bimota Ducati Pantah spine frame

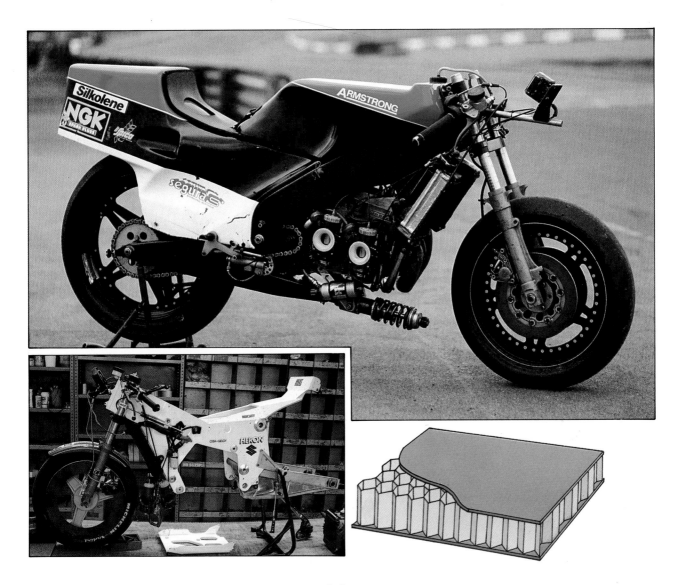

△ Two Grand Prix teams are using frames built from new materials. The Heron Suzuki teams have used sheets of aluminum honeycomb sandwich glued together, but now use a one-piece carbon fiber honeycomb structure. The Armstrong uses a large single spar frame also of carbon fiber. Carbon fiber is stiff and very difficult to damage in a crash.

New materials

Round steel tube is still commonly used for motorcycle frames because it is cheap, easy to cut and join, and very strong. But now aluminum alloy, in tubes of rectangular section, is being used to save weight. Aluminum and even magnesium castings are used for the steering head, swingarm pivot and the swingarm itself.

Plastics are used more and more for fairings, gasoline tanks, mudguards and side panels. Injection-molded, high impact plastics have replaced the more expensive and difficult to produce fiberglass composites. Carbon fiber is immensly strong and very light, and race teams such as Heron Suzuki and Armstrong use frames made from this material. At the moment, carbon fiber is too expensive for road bikes, but this is sure to change.

Production

Like every other high-technology product, motorcycles are now produced by computers and robots. Much design work is done on computers. This enables the designers to decide on the shape, material and size of each part of a new bike, without having to spend lots of time and money on testing. Also the stylists can decide how the new machine will look without having to build lots of models. They simply draw the new bike on a visual display unit linked to a computer. Before a motorcycle goes into production, prototypes are built. These are tested both on the road and in laboratories, so that potential faults can be spotted and eliminated before the new motorcycle goes on sale.

▽ The pictures below are not drawings: they are photographs taken directly from the screen of a visual display unit in the design department of Yamaha's factory. The designer can draw new components with the help of a computer, and the stylist can experiment with different shapes for the bodywork.

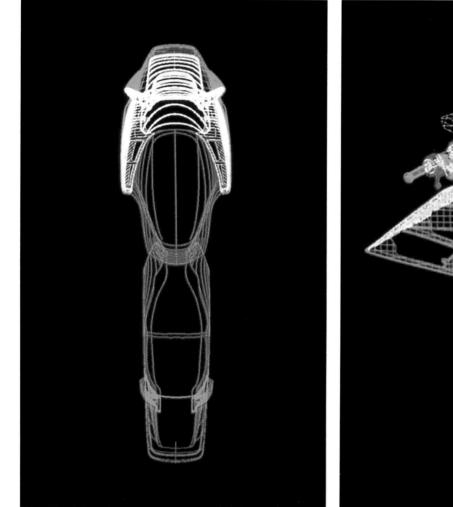

Production lines

Like cars, television sets and most other complex engineering products, motorcycles are produced on production lines. All the big manufacturers have assembly plants that bring together components from outside, specialist suppliers. Heavy castings will come from one factory, tires from another, and instruments such as speedometers from yet another. The assembly line puts all these together, with variations, depending on the country where the bike is to be sold. The finished bike will usually get a short test on a rolling road before being crated up and shipped to the manufacturer's importer in the relevant country, and then to the dealer.

△ The photographs above show three stages of modern motorcycle production at BMW's Berlin factory. Top left, an engine is being run on a test bench in the factory's design and development department. In the main picture, bikes are being assembled on a production line. Top right, a nearly complete machine just off the production line is being run on a rolling road to make sure everything is working properly.

Fun bikes

The great variety of motorcycles today includes bikes that have three wheels as well as two. The sidecar, which used to be humble family transportation, is now a luxury vehicle hitched to a superbike. And sidecars now look like they come from a science-fiction film set, rather than a motorcycle factory. All Terrain Vehicles, or ATVs, started life as cheap cross-country transportation for farmers. Now, however, they are popular as fun bikes and come in sizes from 50cc to race-engined 250cc machines.

Competition motorcycles

The most extreme types of motorcycles are found at drag strips. These machines are designed to cover a quarter of a mile, from a standing start, in the quickest possible time. They have enormous slick rear tires and narrow front tires. They are the fastest motorcycles to travel in a straight line.

▷ Honda's ATC three-wheelers were their best selling products in the USA in 1984. They are great fun, but very difficult to ride compared to an ordinary motorcycle. The insets show the Quasar, which even has a roof on it, and the latest BMW sidecar.

▽ In drag racing anything goes, including rocket-powered bikes like the one in the photograph. Dragsters can actually reach 320 km/h (200 mph) in under seven seconds!

The shape of things to come

Motorcycles are now ready to shake off the design ideas they got from pedal bikes. The loop frame is shrinking and will disappear. The front forks will be replaced by "hub-center steering," operated hydraulically. More lightweight alloys and plastics will be used inside the engine. Developments in ceramics for use as bearings may even mean the production of engines that can run without oil. And automatic gearboxes will become a common feature.

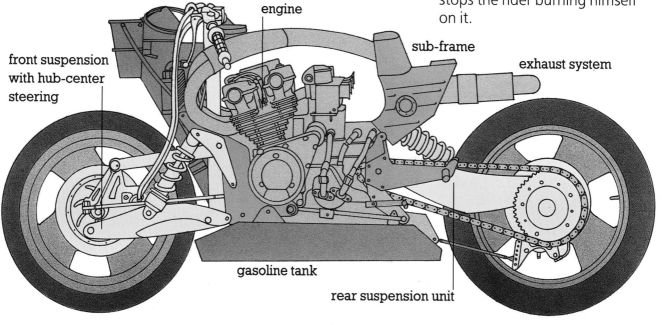

◁ At first glance, this Elf Endurance racer looks like a normal racing bike. However, when stripped of its fairing, as illustrated in the diagram, we can see that it has virtually abandoned its frame altogether! The front and rear suspension systems are attached to the engine by sub-frames. The engine is a four-cylinder Honda four-stroke with the gasoline tank slung underneath the engine. The exhaust system runs over the top of the engine, and a cover stops the rider burning himself on it.

engine

sub-frame

exhaust system

front suspension with hub-center steering

gasoline tank

rear suspension unit

Racing develops the breed

Motorcycle manufacturers test many of their new ideas on the race track before putting them into production. They do this much more quickly than in any other automotive industry. The use of radial tires is the latest example of this.

Honda used their three-cylinder layout in Grand Prix bikes before making a roadster, as did Suzuki with their square-four. The low, light Grand Prix racers with no frames and carbon-fiber bodywork are the most modern machines in motorcycle design. Today's highly developed engines together with these revolutionary chassis are the shape of things to come.

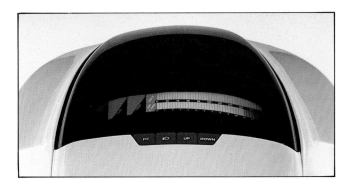

▽ The Falcorustyco is Suzuki's idea of what we will be riding in the 1990s. It has hub-center steering like the Elf, but operated hydraulically from gun-grip handlebars. The dashboard (inset) is totally electronic and you cannot see a chain or shaft final drive, because that too is operated by hydraulic fluid pumped down the swingarm.

Datechart

1885

The first motorized two-wheeler is built by Gottlieb Daimler at Kannstatt in Germany. But it is ten years before the brothers Hildebrand and Alois Wolfmüller build a bike for sale to the public.

1904

FN of Belgium build a four-cylinder motorcycle with shaft drive.

1907

The first Tourist Trophy race, the famous TT, is held on the Isle of Man, UK.

1912

Variable gearing and kickstarters appear for the first time.

1921

A 1000cc Indian (an American V-twin) reaches 160 km/h (100 mph) ridden by D H Davidson. The following year a 500cc Douglas ridden by C G Pullin breaks through the 160 km/h barrier.

1929

Dr Schnuerle invents a system that enables practical two-stroke engines to be produced.

1934

Ernst Henne sets a World Speed Record for two-wheelers at 246 km/h (152.9 mph).

1938

Triumph introduce the Speed Twin, the first of many similar machines with which the British dominate motorcycling for 25 years.

1948

Soichiro Honda produces his first true motorcycle, the 90cc B-type.

1958

The Honda Cub Step-Through is launched. It is still in production in modified form and is the biggest selling two-wheeler in history.

1968

Details of the BSA Rocket/Triumph Trident 750cc triples are released. They win many TTs and the Daytona 200 miles race.

1969

Honda launch the CB750. It is the first of the superbikes, with four overhead-camshaft cylinders set across the frame and a disk brake as standard.

1980

Honda launch the first mass-produced turbocharged motorcycle, the CX500 Turbo.

1985

Suzuki show the Falcorustyco at the Tokyo Motor Show. It is Suzuki's vision of the future, with hydraulic steering and final drive.

Glossary

Crankcases   The main engine cases that house the crankshaft, gearbox and clutch. Usually oil is also held in the cases.

Fairing   Plastic or glass fiber streamlining, which can make the bike aerodynamically efficient and protect the rider from wind.

Fork   The two telescopic legs that steer the front wheel. They are clamped to the wheel axle at the bottom.

Hub-center steering   The front wheel pivots on bearings in its hub and is steered by a linkage to the handlebars.

Ignition   The electrical system that triggers the spark plug(s) at the correct moment to ignite the fuel/air mixture in the cylinder.

Motocross   Racing on enclosed, rough terrain circuits.

Roadracing   Racing on enclosed, macadam roads.

Swingarm   The U-shaped fork that holds the rear wheel in its open end and pivots on an axle that passes through its closed end into bearings in either side of the frame. Sometimes called the swinging arm.

Turbo   A pump driven by exhaust gases that forces extra fuel/air mixture into the engine.

Valves   Small, mushroom shaped components set into the cylinder head. They are opened to allow gas in, "inlet," or out, "exhaust," of a four-stroke engine's cylinders.

Index

Acknowledgments
The publishers wish to thank the following organizations who have helped in the preparation of this book:
BMW (GB) Ltd, Heron Suzuki GB Ltd, Kawasaki, McBain and Paul Agency for Honda, Motorcycle International, Performance Bike, Three Cross (Imports) Ltd, Yamaha-Mitsui and special thanks to Martin Hillier.

Photographic Credits
Cover, contents page and pages 8, 9, 15, 17, 18 (inset), 23, 27 and 28, Kel Edge; title page and page 24, BMW (GB); page 8 (inset) Honda; pages 9, 11 and 29, Motorcycle International; page 13, Suzuki; pages 16, 20 and 21, Jack Burnicle; pages 18, 19 and 26, Garry Stuart; pages 19 and 25, Performance Bike; page 27, Tony Stone Associates.

PRINTED IN BELGIUM BY
proost
INTERNATIONAL BOOK PRODUCTION